Angel of the Odd
Edgar Allan Poe's
Last Days in Philadelphia

*A tale of improbable possibilities
and odd accidents, or, Horror
in the City of Brotherly Love*

Angel of the Odd
Edgar Allan Poe's
Last Days in Philadelphia

A tale of improbable possibilities and odd accidents, or, Horror in the City of Brotherly Love

A. L. Reeser

Front cover:
North Side of Chestnut Street, below Second Street,
Philadelphia, Pennsylvania (1842-1845)
By William Y. McAllister
Library of Congress

Back cover:
Reproduction of the "Ultima Thule" daguerreotype (1848)
Library of Congress

Angel of the Odd: Edgar Allan Poe's Last Days in
Philadelphia
Copyright 2009 by A. L. Reeser

All rights reserved. No part of this book may be reproduced
in any form or by any means, electronic, mechanical, or oral,
including photocopying, recording, or by an information
storage or retrieval system, without permission in writing
from the copyright owner.

1stSight Press
Monocacy, PA

First Printing 2009
Printed in the United States of America
ISBN 978-0-9729265-5-3

Edgar Allan Poe
1809-1849

Mezzotint by William Sartain (1896)
Library of Congress

Table of Contents

Timeline

Map of Philadelphia

Foreword

1. The Fever Called "Living" 1

2. A Literary Hotbed 9

3. Horror in the City of Brotherly Love 17
    Jewelers' Row 17
    Moyamensing 29
    Spring Garden 32
    Fairmount 37
    Northern Liberties 40

4. The Angel of the Odd 53
    Old City 56
    The Premature Burial 59

Afterword 69

Bibliography 73

Selective Timeline

● Denotes activity in Philadelphia

1809	○ Edgar Poe born in Boston, MA, January 19th
1811	○ Poe's birth parents die ○ Taken in by John and Frances Allan of Richmond, VA
1826	○ Enrolls in the University of Virginia
1827	○ Enlists in the Army ○ Moves to Baltimore, MD, and lives with his relatives, the Clemms, and his brother
1830	○ Appointed to the United States Military Academy at West Point
1835	○ Moves to Richmond, VA ○ Editor of the *Southern Literary Messenger*
1836	○ Marries Virginia Eliza Clemm
1837	○ Moves to New York with family
1838	● Moves to Philadelphia, PA, with family
1839	● Editor of *Burton's Gentleman's Magazine*
1840	● Publishes prospectus for "The Penn" in the *Saturday Evening Post*
1841	● Editor of *Graham's Magazine* ● Publishes "The Murders in the Rue Morgue"

1842	• Poe and Dickens meet • Virginia displays symptoms of tuberculosis • Replaced by Rufus Griswold at *Graham's Magazine*
1844	• Poe and family leave Philadelphia for New York
1845	○ Publishes "The Raven" ○ Editor and then owner of *The Broadway Journal* ○ Begins relationship with Frances Osgood ○ "Longfellow War" culminates
1846	○ Publishes "The Literati of New York City"
1847	○ Virginia dies
1848	○ Reconnects with childhood sweetheart, Sarah Elmira Royster ○ Becomes infatuated with Nancy Richmond ○ Briefly engaged to Sarah Helen Whitman

1849	○ Departs New York on June 29th for a southern lecture tour
	  • Arrives in Philadelphia, PA, on June 29th or 30th
	  • Imprisoned at Moyamensing Prison
	  • Arrives at Sartain's house on July 2nd
	  • Visits the Fairmount Water Works
	  • Arrives at Lippard's office on July 12th
	  • Leaves Philadelphia on July 13th
	○ Arrives in Richmond, VA, on July 14th
	○ Engaged to Elmira Royster in July or August
	○ Arrives in Baltimore, MD, on September 28th
	  • Arrives in Philadelphia on September 29th
	○ Hospitalized in Baltimore, MD, on October 3rd
	○ Dies on October 7th

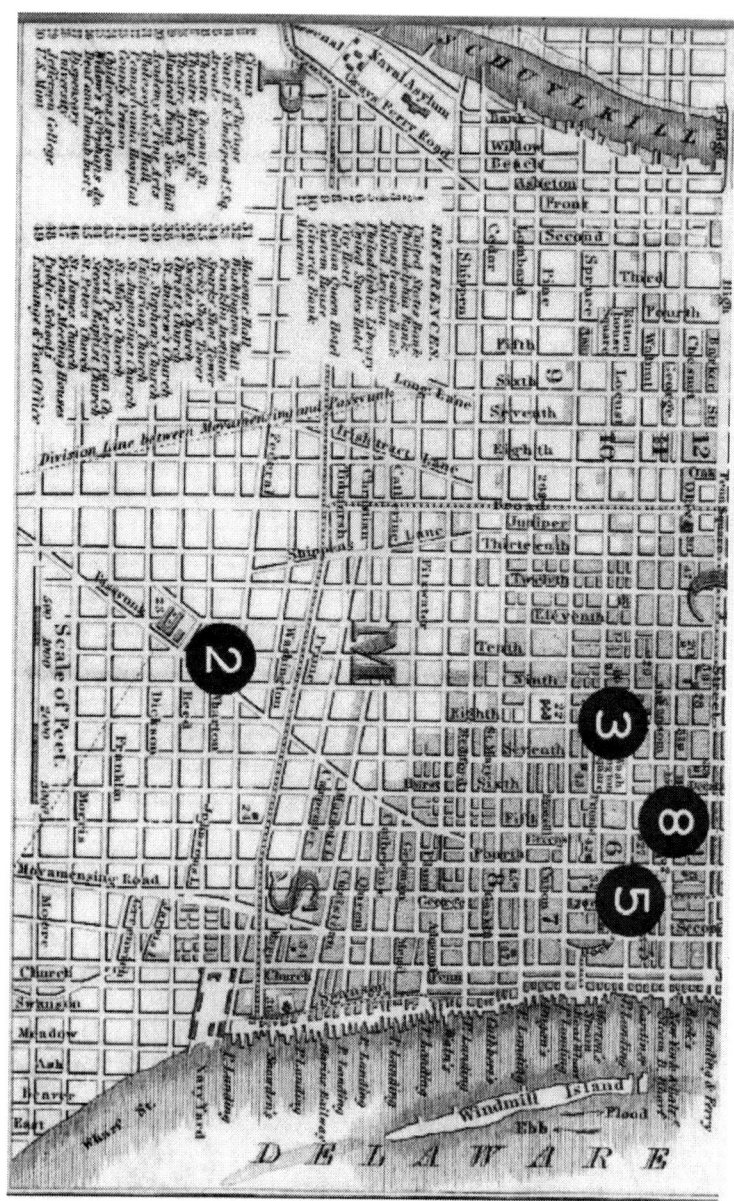

1842 Map of Philadelphia

University of Texas Libraries

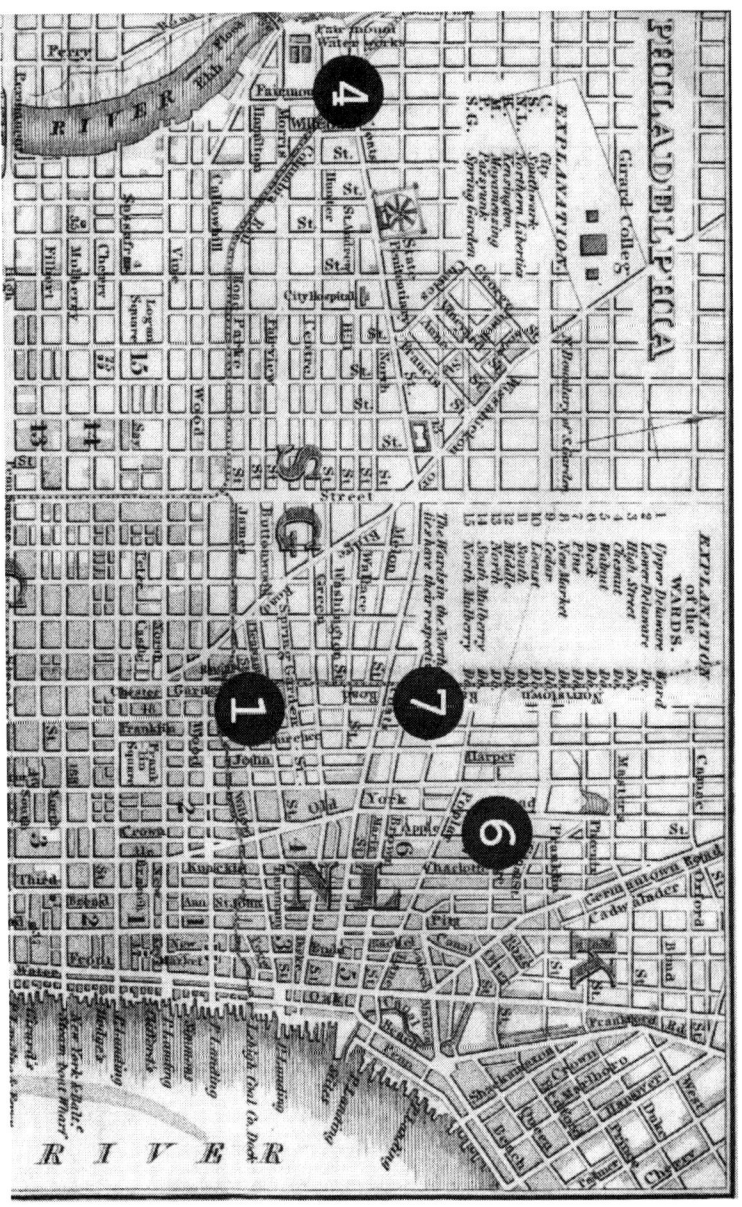

Map Key

❶ Poe's House 1843-44
❷ Moyamensing Prison
❸ John Sartain's House
❹ Fairmount Water Works
❺ George Lippard's Office
❻ George Lippard's House
❼ Charles Chauncey Burr's House
❽ James P. Moss's House

For over 160 years, people have been writing about Edgar Allan Poe. From reviews to gossip, spurious attacks to passionate defenses, biographies to literary critiques, people have been just as fascinated with what he wrote as with who he was. In the year of his bicentennial, 2009, Poe is an American icon: the master of horror and mystery and pioneer of the detective and science fiction genres. He no longer even needs an introduction; a simple raven is enough for people to make the connection.

As for Edgar Allan Poe the man, people have many preconceived ideas about his personal life, most commonly that he was a tortured, tragic poet and/or a neurotic alcoholic. These images, combined with his early death and a century and a half of examination and exaggeration, have transformed mainstream interpretations of him into a character from one of his horror stories. These views by and large stem from people trying to read Poe through his work, seeking biographical answers in his fiction. Often left out of popular versions of him are things such as his penchant for hoaxes, spoofs and satires, and how he had a hand in molding his Byronic image.

But with all that said, as much as Poe's life had its share of ordinariness, his life is also a story of desperation, insanity, love triangles, and perhaps murder. In fact, it is not a stretch to think of his life and death in terms of his detective stories—mystery, plot twists, and an evil nemesis or two. All that is missing is the detective who can piece it all together.

On October 3, 1849, Poe was found disoriented outside a tavern in Baltimore, dressed in someone else's clothes. He died four days later. No one knows how he died—or no one is telling—and no one performed an autopsy. It is one of the greatest mysteries in American history.

What does his death in Baltimore have to do with Philadelphia? Well, the goal of this book is to share the utter strangeness of a two week visit Poe made here in July 1849, just three months before his mysterious death. He was on his way from New York to Richmond, Virginia, for a lecture tour. Along the way, he stopped in Philadelphia. On his return trip from Richmond to New York, he died. In the process of telling this odd story, we will meet some of Poe's acquaintances, both friends and foes, delve into the six years he lived here, and examine his link to Philadelphia. Trivia from his time here and excerpts from pieces he wrote and/or published here appear at the bottom of many of the pages in this book.

In effect, this book is a Poe-centric guide to Philadelphia. By mapping his journey during those two weeks he spent in Philadelphia, we witness the different landmarks and neighborhoods that make up the landscape of this city.

On the other hand, this book is also a Philadelphia-centric guide to Poe, and mapping him is just as interesting, and a lot more difficult. This difficulty stems from the rumor, conjecture, fallacy, and overcorrection that inspire many stories about Poe.

Having written about mysteries his entire life, having invented the modern detective story, Poe probably would appreciate the fact that, 160 years later, we are still trying to figure out the detective story he left us.

According to the methodology of Poe's famous detective, C. August Dupin, sometimes the answer to a mystery is the most obvious one; in other words, when something is in plain sight, it is often overlooked. Other times, the answer hides in the peculiarities. So, in the words of Dupin, "Let us enter into some examinations for ourselves, before we make up an opinion respecting them."

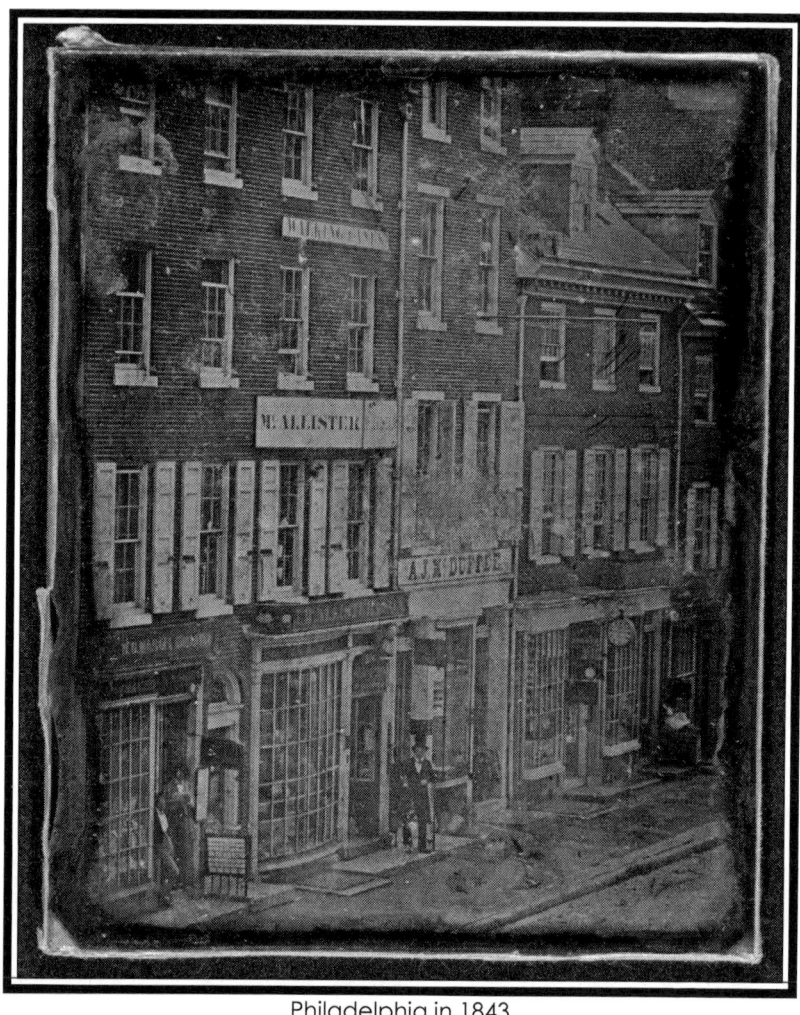

Philadelphia in 1843
Library of Congress

Chapter 1
The Fever Called "Living"

Today, Poe is known as the author of some of the most popular stories of all time. In truth, things were much more complicated for him. He was, as one biographer put it, a "divided" man. At a young age, he seemed to fall in love with a romanticized version of himself, the artist devoted to beauty. But Poe took this pursuit seriously, and he is, in turn, largely considered the first professional American writer. For Poe, however, that meant only one thing: he was poor. One calculation placed his income at only $6,200 for all his writing over 17 years.

Above all, he was devoted to his family: his wife Virginia and his mother-in-law Mrs. Clemm. Together, they did the best they could, moving from Baltimore, to Richmond, to New York, to Philadelphia, and to New York again, while Poe did the best *he* could and tried to make a living doing what he loved.

Some historians view Poe's approach to life as rebellious toward social conventions, painting him as a refined, elegant, Victorian-era mix of Lord Byron, an early

---

At *Graham's Magazine*, Poe was paid $4 per page for critical essays and slightly more for his fiction. *Graham's* paid Longfellow around $50 per poem, and others were paid up to $1,800 for serialized novels. For his editorship there, Poe made $800 per year, a $300 increase from his salary at *Burton's Magazine*.

Angel of the Odd: Edgar Allan Poe's Last Days in Philadelphia

19th century Romantic poet, and Jack Kerouac, a 1950s Beat poet. Poe had talent, a sharp tongue, good looks, and intrigue, especially noticeable, people have written, when you looked into his eyes.

Poe's biographies indicate he helped mold this perception.

> Kindred souls separated by a century, Poe and Jack Kerouac evidently shared a similar approach to handling their manuscripts. Both taped (pasted, in Poe's case) the ends of paper together to create a continuous scroll.

From a young age, he had a habit of constantly re-inventing himself. He used aliases, he embellished his life story, and he loved hoaxes and stretching the truth.

Upon examination, however, these divisions seemed to run deeper and darker, and we are left with two versions of the same man (which, incidentally, was a favorite motif of Poe's), a Jekyll and Hyde-type battle he struggled with throughout his life.

Was he really an alcoholic, or was he adversely affected by just one glass? Did he use drugs, or was it a one time thing? Was he mad, or was he grieving?

Was he, in today's terms, clinically depressed, or did he merely fall "in love with melancholy," as he wrote in a poem? A doctor once suggested Poe had a brain lesion, which could explain mood swings. And some have said he confessed his life-long feelings of isolation when he wrote the lines, "From childhood's hour I have not been / As others were –I have not seen / As others saw...." And still others

---

"For the most wild, yet homely narrative which I am about to pen, I neither expect nor solicit belief. Mad indeed would I be to expect it, in a case where my very senses reject their own evidence. Yet mad am I not—and very surely do I not dream."
"The Black Cat," *United States Saturday Post* (1843)

Angel of the Odd: Edgar Allan Poe's Last Days in Philadelphia

> Rumors circulated that Poe and Virginia secretly married in 1835. In either case, the family voiced their disapproval of the union. It wasn't because Virginia was 13, nor because they were cousins, but rather because they were poor. Rumors also circulated that despite their devotion to each other, they never consummated their marriage.

have said that people just *expect* geniuses to be depressed.

Answers to these questions and more have plagued historians for years. Almost nothing is certain except some biographical facts gleaned from records, and even those are controversial.

Poe was born in Boston, Massachusetts, on January 19, 1809, to actors David and Elizabeth Poe. Orphaned at a young age (David and Elizabeth are rumored to have died within days of each other), Poe was brought into the home of John and Frances Allan, where he was raised as their own child but never formally adopted. Well-schooled both at home and abroad, he eventually made his way to the University of Virginia in 1826, one year after it opened. Within a little over a year, Poe learned of the disappointing engagement of his childhood sweetheart, Sarah Elmira Royster, to another man, he left the University because of gambling debts, he moved to Baltimore to live with the Clemms (relatives on his paternal side), and he joined the Army as Edgar A. Perry.

Over the course of the next several years, Poe published his first book, entered West Point, published two

---

"No one who knows me will doubt that the duty thus self-imposed will be executed to the best of my ability, with all that rigid impartiality, all that cautious examination into facts, and diligent collation of authorities which should ever distinguish him who aspires to the title of historian."
"The Devil in the Belfry," *Saturday Chronicle* (1839)

more books and several stories, and mourned the deaths of his foster parents (and learned he was left out of the will) and the deaths of his older brother and grandmother. In 1835, he secured a job as an editor in Richmond. He left the Clemms briefly, until his cousin, Neilson Poe, reportedly expressed an interest in taking in and caring for their 13-year-old cousin, Virginia. Perhaps to thwart Neilson's proposal, Poe carted her off to Richmond and married her in 1836.

From Richmond, Poe, Virginia (or Sissy, as he called her) and Mrs. Clemm (Virginia's mother and Poe's aunt whom he called Muddy) moved to New York, and then to Philadelphia in 1838, where they spent six years, which would turn out to be the longest time they would spend in one place together.

The Philadelphia that greeted them in 1838 was in a period of transition, as was the rest of the country. Straddling the Jacksonian Era and the antebellum period, the United States at the time was in the throes of the Monroe Doctrine, the Trail of Tears, increased plantation slavery and the Gold Rush. Abraham Lincoln's presidency, as well as the Civil War, was still 20 years away.

In Philadelphia, the 1830s were fairly prosperous times for the upper echelon of society. Pastimes involving bathhouses and pools, botanical gardens, public squares, theater, and sports were commonplace. But by the turn of the decade, simmering problems boiled over. The Bank of the

> "...in general, from the violation of a few simple laws of Humanity, arises the Wickedness of Mankind; ... and that even now— in the present blindness and darkness of all idea on the great question of the Social Condition, it is not impossible that Man, the individual, under certain unusual and highly fortuitous conditions, may be happy." "The Landscape-Garden," *Ladies' Companion* (1842)

United States failed in 1841, and six more banks followed.

The Industrial Revolution had brought numerous factories to the area, but it also brought exploitation of workers. It became increasingly difficult for people to earn a living, and poverty became widespread.

Racial tensions increased in intensity through the 30s and 40s. In 1838, protestors burned down Pennsylvania Hall, run by abolitionists. Although the American Anti-Slavery Society, the Pennsylvania Anti-Slavery Society, and the publication *Pennsylvania Freeman* were located in Philadelphia, the mayor at the time claimed that 99% of his citizens were against abolition.

Economic, ethnic, and religious tensions increased as well. Violence stemming from job competition was common in the 1830s. Friction built up between Protestants and Catholics through the early 1840s, climaxing in 1844, when the worst mob violence in Philadelphia history up to that time

A painting depicting the Nativist Riots in Philadelphia on June 7, 1844.
Poe and his family moved away just two months earlier.
Library of Congress

broke out.

The arts scene also underwent a transition. The 1830s was an amenable decade for artists, including painters, engravers, carvers, sculptors and writers. Magazines such as *Godey's Lady's Book* and *Graham's Magazine* paid their contributors well, up to $12 for 1,000 words and up to $50 for a poem. But by 1844, there was a sense that art appreciation in Philadelphia was fizzling. That year, the Poes, along with many other artists, moved to New York, the burgeoning center of finance and arts.

Poe's first year in New York saw three much publicized events in his career as well as ownership of a magazine. The first event was the publication of his poem, "The Raven." The second was the culmination of Poe's "war" on Boston poet and American sweetheart Henry Wadsworth Longfellow. After around five years of criticizing Longfellow's poems, Poe finally charged him with the dread plagiarism, but with little consequence. The third headline-making event in 1845 was his relationship with poet Frances "Fanny" Osgood. Also in 1845, Poe obtained a position at the *Broadway Journal*. There his duties eventually changed from those of an editor to those of an owner until the magazine went under in January 1846.

Poe's second year in New York saw his increasing alienation from the literary scene with which he had developed a love/hate relationship. In April 1846, he published "The Literati of New York City: Some Honest Opinions at Random Respecting Their Authorial Merits, with

---

In the summer of 1841, while living in Philadelphia, Poe attempted to obtain a government position at the Custom House through the efforts of his friend, Frederick W. Thomas. He did not get the job.

Occasional Words of Personality." The sketches met with great enthusiasm from the public, but the objects of his scorn were less than thrilled and exacted revenge on their heckler. Also this same year, he endured the vengeance of writer Elizabeth Ellet, who saw to it that his relationship with Fanny Osgood became a scandal.

The nature of Poe's last three years can perhaps best be characterized by Virginia's death in January 1847. Following this tragedy, Poe seemed to have lapsed in and out of a prolonged depressive state. Many sources describe this time in Poe's life in terms of bad health, excessive drinking, and mental instability. Even so, he still wrote at least 10 stories, the long essay *Eureka*, over a dozen poems, and numerous articles. Moreover, he continued to publish, to pursue a magazine of his own, and to seek a new wife.

The latter two endeavors would lead him, in a sense, to his death in October 1849.

Written in Philly and published in the *New York Sun*, Poe's "Balloon-Hoax" announced a manned balloon had crossed the Atlantic Ocean. The public believed the story was true, and Poe later remembered the day the story broke: "[T]he whole square surrounding the 'Sun' building was literally besieged ... I never witnessed more intense excitement to get possession of a newspaper."

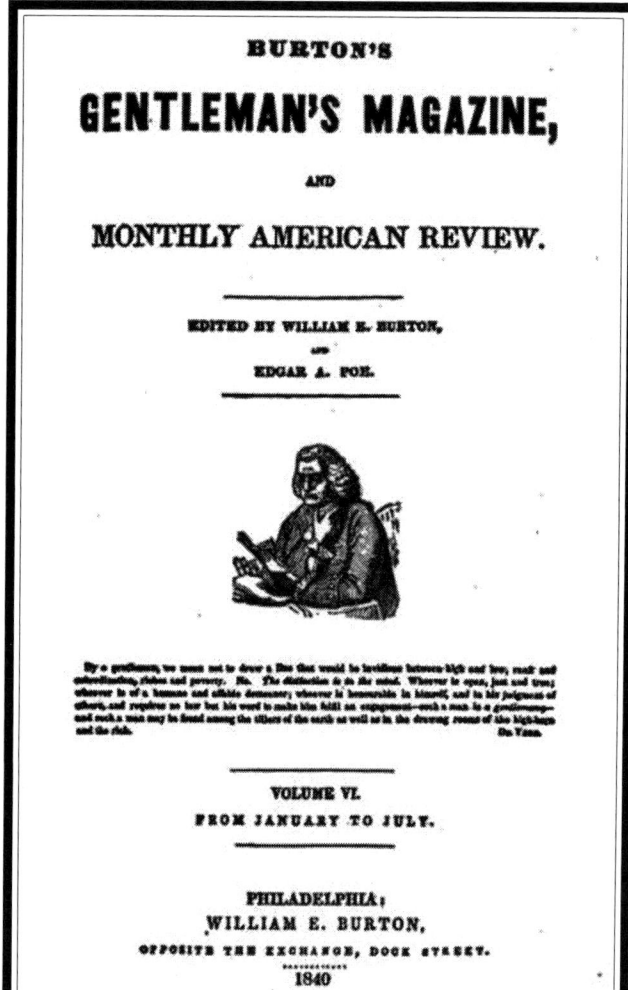

The frontispiece for *Burton's Gentleman's Magazine* in 1840 listing Poe as editor.
The Literary History of Philadelphia (1906)

Chapter 2
A Literary Hotbed

1844 painting of Chestnut Street, location of many printing offices and newspapers, such as *Graham's Magazine* and the *Spirit of the Times*. Philadelphians and visitors promenaded down Chestnut between 3rd and Broad Streets, considered the "Broadway of Philadelphia" in the mid-1800s. *Library of Congress*

Looking back, people say Poe's time in Philadelphia turned out to be his most productive. He wrote some of his most famous stories here: "The Fall of the House of Usher," "The Tell-Tale Heart," "The Black Cat," "The Murders in the Rue Morgue," "The Pit and the Pendulum," "The Gold-Bug," to name only a few. He was associate editor first at *Burton's Gentlemen's Magazine* and then at *Graham's Magazine*, one of the foremost publications in the country. He became a well-known and respected critic with the nickname "Tomahawk Man," and he began to pursue his dream of a literary magazine of the highest esteem devoted to American literature. He originally titled this effort "The Penn," but decided it was too specific to Philadelphia and changed it to "The Stylus."

Modern day view of Chestnut Street between 4th and 5th Streets, where Poe and Charles Dickens met during Dickens's lecture tour of the United States in 1842.

In the center of the American publishing world, Poe's imagination thrived. He published over 30 short stories in Philadelphia, and he developed a reputation for being a "literary wizard."

In fact, Poe took part in one of the most famous literary meetings of all time when he met with the popular English author, Charles Dickens, in Philadelphia. After Poe correctly predicted the end of Dickens's novel, *Barnaby Rudge*, in an ingenious display of his analytical skills, the two expressed an interest in meeting each other. Some think the talking raven in *Barnaby Rudge* partly inspired the raven in Poe's famous poem.

Poe and Dickens met in 1842 at the United States Hotel, which was on Chestnut Street between 4th and 5th Streets. As with most other aspects of Poe's biography, people dispute accounts of their meeting, wondering how congenial the men were to each other. In the interest of countering the effects of the absence of international copyright laws, they made promises to advance the other's career on opposite sides of the Atlantic, but nothing ever happened.

Dickens is just one example of the stature Poe held in the literary world at the time. Without TV, movies, or internet, these people were almost the celebrities of their time. And Poe counted as his friends some of the most successful people in the publishing industry.

One of these friends was George Rex Graham, editor of *Graham's Magazine*, which was located just down the street from the United States Hotel at the southeast corner of Chestnut and 3rd Streets.

In April 1841, two months after Poe became editor there, *Graham's* published "The Murders in the Rue Morgue," the first of his tales of ratiocination (i.e. reasoning) and the first modern detective story. The characteristics of the story, as well as the detective character, C. August Dupin,

---

Scholars have also pointed to another source of inspiration for "The Raven": a bird shop in Philly owned by Poe's friend Henry Beck Hirst, an attorney and poet. Hirst insisted until he died that the two of them wrote the poem together while hanging out at Hirst's shop with his pet raven. Hirst was institutionalized at the end of his life at Blocksley Almshouse in West Philadelphia.

would be echoed by authors again and again, most notably in Sir Arthur Conan Doyle's Sherlock Holmes.

Besides being written and published in Philadelphia, "The Murders in the Rue Morgue" has other ties to the city. Inspiration is said to have come from an orangutan on display at the Philadelphia Masonic Hall, and the manuscript made its way to Drexel Institute in the late 1800s, then to Colonel Richard Gimble's collection, and finally to the Free Library of Philadelphia.

Poe left his post at *Graham's* in May 1842, but it became, in some ways, the nexus of many of Poe's problems over the next few years and even after his death. The reason why Poe left the magazine remains unclear. Some attribute his resignation to problems with co-editor Charles J. Peter, and others point to Rufus Griswold, a writer and critic who joined the staff at *Graham's* at the same time Poe resigned. According to Poe, "My reason for resigning was disgust with the namby-pamby character of the Magazine—a character which it was impossible to eradicate. I allude to the contemptible pictures, fashion-plates, music, and love-tales. The salary, moreover, did not pay me for the labour which I was forced to bestow."

Griswold became a complicated figure in Poe's life. If truth be told, it seems not many people liked him; they claim that he was egotistical and arrogant without having much reason and that he was manipulative. Whether he and Poe liked each other is debatable. Some have said they did nothing more than tolerate each other. Nevertheless, Poe

---

To share his fascination with the way the mind works, Poe challenged Philadelphia readers to send him their coded messages to see if he could decipher them—he always won. Scholars still debate the extent of Poe's cryptology ability.

allegedly put Griswold in charge of his literary estate just months before he died.

Before Poe left *Graham's*, he made the acquaintance of Frances Osgood. In March 1842, Osgood made her first contribution to the magazine with her story "May Evelyn." In 1845, the two began a public "literary courtship." Both were married at the time, but they began to publish romantic poems back and forth, dedicating them to each other, and making headlines in the process. Some swear that this banter was the extent of their flirtation.

Frances Sargent Osgood
The American Female Poets (1848)

But scandal followed, and poet Elizabeth Ellet, who had also contributed to *Graham's Magazine*, fed the flames. Her notorious interference began after Poe snubbed her advances, and her revenge ranged from telling everyone that Poe was a womanizer and a drunk to speculating that Fanny's third child was Poe's.

In addition to its "Page 6" quality, the Osgood/Ellet story shows Poe's multi-faceted personality. Apparently, while visiting the Poes, Ellet happened to notice letters from Osgood addressed to Poe. Certain that these letters placed

Poe reportedly met T.D. English in 1839 at the corner of 6th and Chestnut Streets in Philadelphia. They shared an interest in phrenology, the subject of English's thesis at the University of Pennsylvania's School of Medicine.

Elizabeth Fries Ellet
Cyclopaedia of American Literature (1856)

Osgood in a compromising position, Ellet urged her to demand their return. Upon hearing of Ellet's instructions, Poe retorted that *Ellet* should "look after her *own* letters" before worrying about Osgood's, and he returned them to her. His jab so effectively embarrassed Ellet that she sent her brother to demand Poe give up her letters, which Poe could not do since he had already sent them to her. Following this blow-up with Ellet's brother, Poe turned to Thomas Dunn English, an acquaintance at the time and fellow writer, in hopes of securing a hand gun. English, however, did not believe Ellet had ever written any letters and refused to help Poe. That was the end of their friendship.

In an unfortunate choice of words, Poe apologized for the episode by claiming temporary insanity. Ellet latched on to this explanation, spreading rumors that Poe was insane, a story that was picked up by newspapers nationwide. Her grudge against Poe lasted the rest of his life.

By all accounts, Ellet was not the only one to resent Poe. Rufus Griswold, Poe's replacement at *Graham's*, fruitlessly vied for Fanny's affection during her dalliance

---

During Poe's first year at *Graham's*, he published his "Autography" series, in which he analyzed the signatures of popular authors. Of Ellet's, he said signatures like hers "seldom evince high originality or very eminent talent of any kind."

> In 1846, Poe began publishing "The Literati of New York," which featured sharp sketches of current writers. The sketch of T. D. English prompted a series of no-holds-barred retaliations by English and others that attacked Poe personally and professionally. The battle culminated in Poe bringing a lawsuit for libel against the *Evening Mirror*, the publication that printed them. He was awarded $225.

with Poe. Some people point to this competition as the start of Griswold's animosity toward Poe.

Whatever the root of the problem, Griswold remains responsible, in part, for the odd evolution of Poe's legacy. Upon Poe's death, he rewrote and outright created parts of Poe's history, a vilification that informed people's opinions of Poe for over a century. He also added the seemingly innocuous "Allan" to Poe's name. When Poe was alive, he never used "Allan," at most he used just the initial. This omission was intended as a pointed break from John Allan, his estranged foster father. Some believe Griswold distorted Poe's biography as revenge from a bad review Poe might have wrote; others cite the Osgood affair or the professional rivalry at *Graham's Magazine* in Philadelphia.

The reason behind Poe and Griswold's strange arrangement has been much debated. Why would Poe want his arch enemy to be in charge of his literary estate? Did Poe

> "There are some secrets which do not permit themselves to be told. Men die nightly in their beds, wringing the hands of ghostly confessors, and looking them piteously in the eyes—die with despair of heart and convulsion of throat, on account of the hideousness of mysteries which will not *suffer themselves* to be revealed. Now and then, alas, the conscience of man takes up a burthen so heavy in horror that it can be thrown down only into the grave. And thus the essence of all crime is undivulged." "The Man of the Crowd," *Casket* and *Burton's Gentleman's Magazine* (1840)

ever really appoint him? If he had, was it really an unusual request, considering many authors of the time appointed Griswold in the same role? Either way, tradition has it that Poe asked him to be his executor in the summer of 1849, in case, Poe allegedly said, of his unexpected death.

Rufus Wilmot Griswold
The Poets and Poetry of America (1855)

Griswold's love life was riddled with trouble. After his first wife died young, he remarried, only to find his new bride "incapable of being a wife" on their wedding night. Much speculation exists about the meaning of this claim. Nevertheless, he divorced her, and remarried someone else. Not to be outdone, his second wife appealed the divorce (at the urging of Elizabeth Ellet), at which point his third wife divorced him.

In Poe's analysis of Griswold's signature, he wrote that it "is by no means a good one. It appears unformed, and vacillates in a singular manner; so that nothing can be predicated from it, except a certain unsteadiness of purpose."

Chapter 3
Horror in the City of Brotherly Love

The summer of 1849 is when we pick up the story of Poe's two week journey in Philadelphia. That year, Poe was residing with Mrs. Clemm in Fordham, New York. He was pursuing his magazine and searching for a new companion. Virginia had passed away in 1847 after a long struggle with tuberculosis, and he seemed intent on finding a replacement. To raise subscription money and to revisit his childhood sweetheart, he departed from New York for Richmond, Virginia. Philadelphia was not on the itinerary, but he stopped here nonetheless.

His stopover in Philadelphia lasted only two weeks, but during that time, he endured a series of bizarre events that people have never figured out. Just three short months later, he was dead.

JEWELERS' ROW

Most historians agree it was July 2nd when Poe unexpectedly surfaced at the home of his friend John Sartain, which was located on Sansom Street between 7th and 8th Streets, today's Jewelers' Row. Considered the best American engraver of

A drawing of the 700 block of Sansom Street, looking east from 8th Street, from the turn of the 20th century.
Library of Congress

the time, Sartain did the illustrations for *Graham's Magazine*, and later had his own magazine, *Sartain's Union Magazine*, located on the northwest corner of 3rd and Walnut Streets.

Most important for our purposes is a memoir Sartain wrote when he was in his late eighties, *Reminiscences of a Very Old Man*. From this, we learn of Poe's arrival at his house, 50 years earlier.

Poe told Sartain he got off the train in Bordentown, New Jersey, but returned to Philadelphia in mortal fear. Sartain remembered the strange event as follows:

> The last time I saw Mr. Poe was late in that same year, 1849, and then under such peculiar and almost fearful conditions that the experience can never fade from my memory. Early one Monday afternoon he suddenly entered my engraving room, looking pale and haggard, with a wild and frightened expression in his eyes. I did not let him see that I noticed it, and shaking him cordially by the hand invited him to be seated, when he began, "Mr. Sartain, I have come to you for a refuge and protection; will you let me stay with you? It is necessary to my safety that I lie concealed for a time." I assured him that he was welcome, that in my house he would be perfectly safe, and he could stay as long as he liked, but I asked him what was the matter. He said it would be difficult for me to believe what he had to tell, or that such things were possible in this nineteenth century. I made him as comfortable as I could, and then proceeded with my work, which was pressing. After he

John Sartain
Philadelphia and Popular Philadelphians (1891)

had had time to calm down a little, he told me that he had been on his way to New York, but he had overheard some men who sat a few seats back of him plotting how they should kill him and then throw him off from the platform of the car. He said they spoke so low that it would have been impossible for him to hear and understand the meaning of their words, had it not been that his sense of hearing was so wonderfully acute. They could not guess that he heard them, as he sat so quiet and apparently indifferent to what was going on, but when the train arrived at the Bordentown station he gave them the slip and remained concealed until the cars moved on again. He had returned to Philadelphia by the first train back, and hurried to me for refuge.

I told him that it was my belief the whole scare was the creation of his own fancy, for what interest could those people have in taking his life, and at such risk to themselves? He said, "It was revenge." "Revenge for what?" said I. He answered, "Well, a woman trouble."

Now and then some fragmentary conversation passed between us as I engraved, and shortly I began to perceive a singular change in the current of his thoughts. From such fear of assassination his mind gradually veered round to an idea of self-destruction, and his words clearly indicated this tendency. After a long silence he said suddenly, "If this mustache of mine were removed I should not be so readily recognized; will you lend me a razor, that I may shave it off?" I told him that as I never shaved I had no razor, but if he wanted it removed I could readily do it for him with scissors. Accordingly I took him to the bathroom and performed the operation successfully.

One possible inconsistency in Sartain's account is his claim that Poe was traveling to New York, not from New York. Readers have interpreted this either as Sartain's mistake, Poe's intentional or unintentional mistake, or, perhaps, the truth.

Readers also have puzzled over the incident with Poe's moustache. People in Richmond reportedly saw Poe with a fully grown moustache two weeks later. What would Sartain gain by including this detail were it not true? Had the moustache merely grown back by the time Poe got to Richmond? Another explanation is that the accounts from Richmond were actually several weeks, not two, after this incident.

One incident Poe apparently did not mention to Sartain, but that we learn of from a letter, was that Poe lost his satchel and later found it at the train depot. According to a letter he wrote to Mrs. Clemm after arriving in Richmond on July 14th, nothing but the lectures he planned to present were stolen:

"True!—nervous—very, very dreadfully nervous I had been and am; but why will you say that I am mad? The disease had sharpened my senses—not destroyed—not dulled them. Above all was the sense of hearing acute. I heard all things in the heaven and in the earth. I heard many things in hell. How, then, am I mad? Hearken! and observe how healthily, how calmly, I can tell you the whole story."
"The Tell-Tale Heart," *Boston Pioneer* (1843)

Oh, Mother, I am *so* ill while I write—but I resolved that come what would, I would not sleep again without easing your dear heart as far as I could.

My valise was lost for ten days. At last I found it at the depot in Philadelphia, but (you will scarcely credit it) they had opened it and stolen *both lectures*. Oh, Mother, think of the blow to me this evening, when on examining the valise, these lectures were gone. All my object here is over unless I can recover them or re-write one of them.

Poe's stolen lectures were reportedly never recovered, and no one knows what they were about. When he finally delivered his lecture in Richmond in August, it was one he had previously given.

If we believe Poe's account, could this theft have been related to the men he said were plotting his murder? Poe wielded his pen like a sword, maiming literary careers left and right. He also lashed out at international copyright laws. If Poe's lectures were no longer in his possession, theoretically anyone could lay claim to authoring them.

Maria Clemm
American Bookmen
(1898)

"There are few persons, even among the calmest thinkers, who have not occasionally been startled into a vague yet thrilling half-credence in the supernatural, by *coincidences* of so seemingly marvellous a character that, as *mere* coincidences, the intellect has been unable to receive them."
"The Mystery of Marie Roget," *Ladies' Companion* (1842)

Angel of the Odd: Edgar Allan Poe's Last Days in Philadelphia

Marie Louise Shew
Edgar Allan Poe Society of Baltimore

Nancy Richmond, Poe's "Annie"
Edgar Allan Poe Society of Baltimore

Sarah Helen Whitman
Life of Edgar Allan Poe (1903)

Sarah Elmira Royster
Edgar Allan Poe Society of Baltimore

"Some persons ridicule the idea of 'love at first sight'; but those who think clearly, not less than those who feel deeply, have always advocated its existence."
"The Spectacles," *Dollar Newspaper* (1844)

Poe, however, believed the men were following him because they sought revenge for a woman trouble. That explanation could lead us in many directions.

Shortly before and then after Virginia's death, Poe's relationships with women became complex and, more often than not, hard to define.

Some of his women friends were what we could call colleagues. To help make ends meet, Poe would publicly endorse select women writers by publishing favorable reviews of their work. Poe apparently hated having to accept these nominal kickbacks, which Mrs. Clemm sometimes arranged. His feelings are clear in his description of these women as a "heartless, unnatural, venomous, dishonorable set."

> "Hear the mellow wedding bells—Golden bells!
> What a world of happiness their harmony foretells!
> Through the balmy air of night
> How they ring out their delight!"
> - From "The Bells," published in the months after Poe's death in *Sartain's Union Magazine*

But it seems Poe was a romantic at heart. In the year before he died, he tried to marry at least four women, all the while mourning Virginia.

Marie Louise Shew became Poe's first attempt at remarrying. She cared for the Poes during and after Virginia's death, and it was not long before Poe began having feelings for her. Her only reciprocation was kindness and some lines of his poem, "The Bells." In a heartbreaking

---

"That Ligeia loved me, I should not have doubted; and I might have been easily aware that, in a bosom such as hers, love would have reigned no ordinary passion. But in death only, was I fully impressed with the intensity of her affection."
"Ligeia," *American Museum* (1838)

letter to her, he bemoans her rejection of him: "[A]nd for me alas! unless some true and tender and pure womanly love saves me, I shall hardly last a year longer, alone! a few short months, will tell, how far my strength—(physical, and moral) will carry me in life here."

About a month after penning that letter, Poe met Mrs. Nancy Locke Richmond. Some say she was his second true love after Virginia, but, unfortunately for Poe, "Annie," as he called her, was married. They reportedly met in 1848 during Poe's lecture tour, after which Poe wrote scores of letters to her. People do not know if their relationship was ever more than a friendship, but Mr. Richmond did put an end to things when Jane Locke, a neighbor and relative of the Richmonds who was smitten with Poe, started the rumor mill to sabotage the situation, á la Elizabeth Ellet.

> In the mid-1800s, Spiritualism was thoroughly embedded in religious and social life. People conjured spirits from the afterlife at séances both public and private, celebrating their immortality with spirit communication.

At the same time, Poe was courting Sarah Helen Whitman, a widow six years older than him, who was friends with Fanny Osgood. Poe and Whitman found common ground in pop culture, attending weekly séances and talking about Spiritualism, mesmerism, and phrenology. They were also intellectual equals. They both traveled in fashionable literary circles, but Whitman's circle was comprised of Poe's rivals, the Transcendentalists,

---

"Some one *did* introduce me to the gentleman, I am sure—at some public meeting, I know very well—held about something of great importance, no doubt—and at some place or other, of this I feel convinced—whose name I have unaccountably forgotten." "The Man that was Used Up," *Burton's Gentleman's Magazine* (1839)

which was an obstacle they never overcame. In addition, Helen remained cautious because of warnings from women who did not like Poe, one of them being Elizabeth Ellet.

During their courtship, in November 1848, Poe might have attempted suicide by overdose, an event dubbed the "laudanum episode." Many believe it was only accidental, but others cite his violent imagery in correspondence to her as precursors to a suicide attempt. Soon after, Helen did finally agree to marry him, even agreeing to forfeit her inheritance at her family's request. She had one condition: he had to swear off alcohol. He couldn't. She called off the wedding just days before it was scheduled to take place. Despite their romantic falling out, she was a staunch defender of him after he died, doing damage control after Griswold's biographical hatchet job.

Finally, Poe courted Sarah Elmira Royster, his childhood sweetheart. Having first reunited with her a year earlier, he planned to meet with her again upon his arrival in Richmond.

Some people have been surprised to learn of Poe in the middle of so many romantic entanglements. When "The Raven" was published in 1845, literary genius/tortured artist Poe became dreamboat Poe. He became an overnight sensation, garnering recognition if not wealth—he only made $15 from its first publishing. Much like today, people then were enthralled with the afterlife, particularly the possibility of contacting loved ones who had passed away. "The Raven"

> "Yes; I have made history. My fame is universal. It extends to the uttermost ends of the earth. You cannot take up a common newspaper in which you shall not see some allusion to the immortal Thingum Bob." "The Literary Life of Thingum Bob, Esq.,"
> *Southern Literary Messenger* (1844)

rode this wave of paranormal popularity, and women fell in love with the mysterious man in black who wrote it.

Most scholars believe Poe began composing "The Raven" while he lived in Philadelphia. It was published in January 1845, about a year after he moved away. In any case, Philadelphia still pays homage to the poem, by way of the Free Library of Philadelphia, at 19th and Vine Streets. Here resides Charles Dickens's pet raven, Grip, who was reportedly the inspiration for *Barnaby Rudge* and Poe's "The Raven." Dickens was so affectionate toward his bird that he had it stuffed when it died, and it now calls Philadelphia home.

The Central branch of the Free Library of Philadelphia, located at 19th and Vine Streets, houses a remarkable and rare collection of Poe artifacts, from manuscripts to portraits.

So which "woman trouble" was Poe referring to that desperate day at Sartain's house? His thwarted engagement to Sarah Helen Whitman stirred up plenty of trouble, as did his relationship with Annie, and Elizabeth Ellet still had not recovered from Poe's cold shoulder. In Poe's own opinion, "Hell hath no fury like a woman scorned."

Angel of the Odd: Edgar Allan Poe's Last Days in Philadelphia

"The Raven" has proven as immortal as Poe.
Pictured here is a 1908 theater poster of
"The Raven: The Love Story of Edgar Allan Poe,"
by George Hazelton and starring Henry Ludlowe.
Library of Congress

In 1843, Poe won $100 when he entered his story "The Gold Bug" in a competition by the Philadelphia *Dollar Newspaper*. After the success of "The Raven," Poe compared the two pieces: "The bird beat the bug, though, all hollow."

MOYAMENSING

Moyamensing Prison
Library of Congress

Known as the Philadelphia County Prison, Moyamensing was built in 1835 between 10th and Reed Streets and Passyunk Avenue. The Gothic-style structure had a debtors' prison next to it, made of red sandstone with Egyptian-style construction. Notorious serial killer Herman Webster Mudget was hung at Moyamensing in 1896. It closed in 1963.

Sartain Street runs sporadically through the length of Philadelphia, from Oregon Avenue in South Philadelphia to the West Kensington neighborhood of North Philadelphia. Will Philly one day boast a Poe Street?

Before we reviewed Poe's romances, we left Poe and Sartain at Sartain's house in Jewelers' Row, just a few days into Poe's two week journey. From Sartain's, they waited for the omnibus at 9th and Chestnut Streets after Poe expressed a desire to go "to the Schuylkill." While they waited, Poe made Sartain promise that the portrait Fanny had painted of him would go to Mrs. Clemm upon his death. Poe and Osgood's relationship evidently developed into a life-long friendship.

In addition to believing men were following him, Poe also told Sartain he was incarcerated at Moyamensing Prison in South Philadelphia almost immediately upon his arrival on June 29th or 30th.

No records exist of Poe's confinement there, but as Poe told it, all charges against him were dropped when the mayor recognized him as "Poe, the poet." Sartain heard confirmation of this story later, independently corroborating Poe's account. And, according to Poe, he *was* there—and it was because he tried to use counterfeit money, even though Sartain believed it was for drinking one too many.

Poe also references his imprisonment in a letter to Mrs. Clemm postmarked July 7th:

New York, July 7.

My dear, dear Mother,

I have been *so* ill—have had the cholera, or spasms quiet as bad, and can now hardly hold the pen . . .

The very instant you get this, *come* to me. The joy of seeing you will almost compensate for our sorrows. We can but die together. It *is* no use to reason with me *now;* I must die. I have no desire to live since I have done "Eureka." I could accomplish nothing more. For your sake it would be sweet to live, but we must die together. You have been all in all to me, darling, ever beloved mother, and dearest, truest friend.

I was never *really* insane, except on occasions where my heart was touched . . .

I have been taken to prison once since I came here for [getting] drunk; but *then I* was not. It was about Virginia.

One biographer described Poe's work as concealing and revealing at the same time. We can probably say the same thing about his personal correspondence as well.

> "Looking upward, I surveyed the ceiling of my prison. It was some thirty or forty feet overhead, and constructed much as the side walls. In one of its panels a very singular figure riveted my whole attention. It was the painted figure of Time as he is commonly represented, save that, in lieu of a scythe, he held what, at a casual glance, I supposed to be the pictured image of a huge pendulum such as we see on antique clocks."
> "The Pit and the Pendulum," *The Gift* (1842)

Poe postmarks this letter from New York on the 7th. While his activity in Philadelphia is uncertain, it is generally agreed that he was here—somewhere—on that date. Was it simply a mistake? Again, readers have wondered whether the New York reference was a mistake. Some see it as evidence of Poe's paranoia, and others see it as symptomatic of cholera. Because of inadequate treatment of drinking water, Philadelphia was two months into a cholera epidemic in July 1849. Yet Poe claims to "have had the cholera, *or spasms quite as bad*" (emphasis added). Would an intestinal disease that causes vomiting, cramps and dehydration also cause hallucinations like he experienced? Perhaps, if he had a severe case of it.

SPRING GARDEN

Poe does not mention cholera in the letter again. Instead, he attributes his delirium to emotional reasons—"when his heart was touched." His imprisonment, he says, had nothing to do with drinking, but rather with Virginia. We could take this admission to mean the state, since he was on his way there, or his late wife. The latter perhaps makes more sense.

Is it any wonder that Virginia would have weighed so heavily on his mind during this trip in 1849? She died just two years earlier, and she first showed symptoms of her

---

"I grant, at least, that there are two distinct conditions of my mental existence—the condition of a lucid reason, not to be disputed, ...; and a condition of shadow and doubt, appertaining to the present, and to the recollection of what constitutes the second great era of my being." "Eleonora," *The Gift* (1841)

An idealized rendition of the Poe House on 7th Street? The handwritten caption reads "House where Poe wrote The Raven 1840." *Library of Congress*

sickness while they lived in Philadelphia. Evidently, Virginia was singing at their house, perhaps at Poe's 33rd birthday party, when she began bleeding from her mouth. She was bedridden for the next two weeks in a small room with a low ceiling. Friends remembered the tension in the room, with Poe unable to handle any mention of death. Poe would later confess the toll her sickness took on him: "I became insane, with long intervals of horrible sanity. During these fits of absolute unconsciousness I drank, God only knows how often or how much. As a matter of course, my enemies referred the insanity to the drink rather than the drink to the insanity. I had indeed, nearly abandoned all hope of a permanent cure when I found one in the *death* of my wife. This I can & do endure as becomes a man—it was the horrible never-ending oscillation between hope & despair which I could not longer have endured without total loss of reason."

Angel of the Odd: Edgar Allan Poe's Last Days in Philadelphia

Virginia Eliza Clemm Poe
Edgar Allan Poe Society of Baltimore

An unknown artist painted this portrait after Virginia had died. Readers see "The Masque of the Red Death" and "The Oval Portrait" as written in response to Virginia taking sick in 1842. In the first, the color red factors heavily as a symbol of blood, and "death" is the uninvited guest at a ball. In the second, an artist brings about the death of his model as he paints her.

"My first recollection of the Poes is of one of us little children singing the old song Gaffer Poe to pretty Mrs. Poe. …'Mr. Poe was a man of great riches and fame. And I loved him, I'm sure, though I liked not his name. He asked me to wed. In a rage I said No, I'll never marry you and be called Mrs. Poe.'"
Anne E.C. Clarke, from Sartain's *Reminiscences*

Angel of the Odd: Edgar Allan Poe's Last Days in Philadelphia

Edgar Allan Poe National Historic Site at 530 N. 7th Street

The Poes' only surviving residence is located at 7th and Spring Garden Streets. Poe enthusiast Richard Gimble opened the house as a museum in 1933, and then left it to the city when he died. The house reopened in 1980 as the Edgar Allan Poe National Historic Site. As it is pictured here, the house on the right is the entrance to the site, which actually would have been the Poes' neighbor. Their residence was behind this house. The Poes also lived near 2nd and Arch Streets, 16th and Locust Streets, and 25th and Fairmount Streets.

> "The whole company, indeed, seemed now deeply to feel that in the costume and bearing of the stranger neither wit nor propriety existed. The figure was tall and gaunt, and shrouded from head to foot in the habiliments of the grave. The mask which concealed the visage was made so nearly to resemble the countenance of a stiffened corpse that the closest scrutiny must have had difficulty in detecting the cheat." "The Masque of the Red Death," *Graham's Magazine* (1842) as "The Mask of the Red Death"

Angel of the Odd: Edgar Allan Poe's Last Days in Philadelphia

Visitors claim a likeness between the basement of the Spring Garden house, pictured here, and the one in the short story "The Black Cat." In this story, a man places the corpses of his wife and cat in the walls of his basement.

A raven perches outside the Spring Garden house. The Poes and their cat, Catterina, lived here from 1843 to 1844. It was their last Philadelphia home.

"And then the brush was given, and then the tint was placed; and, for one moment, the painter stood entranced before the work which he had wrought; but in the next, while he yet gazed, he grew tremulous and very pallid, and aghast, and crying with a loud voice 'This is indeed Life itself!' ..." "The Oval Portrait," *Graham's Magazine* as "Life in Death" (1842)

 FAIRMOUNT

Poe and Sartain took the omnibus to a stop on Callowhill Street, just short of Fairmount Avenue. The only light when they disembarked came from the open door of a tavern that stood on the corner by the bus stop. They proceeded to walk into the darkness—"pitchy dark" is how Sartain described it—until they reached a long, steep flight of wooden steps that led to the top of a reservoir, which stood on a nearby hill called Faire Mount (hence the name Fairmount Park). This was not an unusual trek to make—in their day, the grounds of the Water Works, which sit on the Schuylkill River off modern-day Kelly Drive, were a premier tourist destination.

> The Fairmount Water Works was a wonder of technology and aesthetics to 19th century visitors. Construction began in 1812 to supply the city with potable water, using the Schuylkill River and the reservoir which sat atop Fair Mount. The acquisition of more land for a public park and the cultivation of gardens and an esplanade made the Water Works a unique experience. Its popularity and usefulness started to decline around 1850, only a year after Poe's story unfolded there.

As they walked through that darkness, Sartain remembered how he kept himself between Poe and the water, fearing for Poe's life and his own, thinking that Poe might suddenly fling himself over the edge with his friend in his arms. Sartain's fears were only exacerbated by the stories that Poe told him that night.

"There is no just ground, therefore, for the charge brought against me by certain ignoramuses—that I have never written a moral tale, or, in more precise words, a tale with a moral." "Never Bet the Devil Your Head," *Graham's Magazine* (1841)

Sitting side by side, Poe confided the bizarre events he thought had happened to him at Moyamensing Prison, his utterances as "calm, deliberate, [and] measured" as if they were facts.

Fairmount Water Works. *Library of Congress*
The steep incline on the left was the hill leading to the reservoir.
Poe and Sartain would have approached it from the opposite side.

If his imprisonment was real, his experiences there were only figments of his imagination:

> "I was confined in a cell in Moyamensing Prison," said he, "and through my grated window was visible the battlemented granite tower. On the topmost stone of the parapet, between the embrasures, stood perched against the dark sky a young female brightly radiant, like silver dipped in light, either in herself or in her environment, so that the cross-bar shadows thrown from my window were distinct on the opposite wall. From this

position, remote as it was, she addressed to me a series of questions in words not loud but distinct, and I dared not fail to hear and make apt response. Had I failed once either to hear or to make pertinent answer, the consequences to me would have been something fearful; but my sense of hearing wonderfully acute, so that I passed safely through this ordeal, which was a snare to catch me. But another was in store.

"An attendant asked me if I would like to take a stroll about the place, I might see something interesting, and I agreed. In the course of our rounds on the ramparts we came to a cauldron of boiling spirits. He asked me if I would not like to take a drink. I declined, but had I said yes, what do you suppose would have happened?" I said I could not guess. "Why, I should have been lifted over the brim and dipped into the hot liquid up to the lip, like Tantalus." "Yes," said I, "but that would have killed you." "Of course it would," said he, "that's what they wanted; but you see, again I escaped the snare. So at last, as a means to torture me and wring my heart, they brought out my mother, Mrs. Clemm, to blast my sight by seeing them first saw off her feet at the ankles, then her legs to the knees, her thighs at the hips, and so on."

He stopped telling the story to Sartain then, as convulsions

When Poe lived in Philadelphia, he and Henry Beck Hirst spent a lot of time at Thomas Cottrell Clarke's house at 12th and Walnut Streets. For a short period of time, Clarke partnered with Poe to publish Poe's magazine. The two reportedly decided to change the name from "The Penn" to "The Stylus."

shook him too hard for him to finish. They continued to sit together; Poe lost in his memories of that horrible night, and Sartain intent on returning his friend safely home.

On their way back to the bus stop, Sartain took equal care to continue the conversation and to keep Poe away from the water, so unsteady was Poe's step and frame of mind. Any additional strange and fantastical things Poe might have confided are lost to an old man's memory. The next thing Sartain tells us is that once they reached the house, Poe slept on a sofa in the dining room, and Sartain slept alongside him across three chairs.

Two days after their walk to the Water Works, Sartain felt Poe had regained enough composure to go out by himself (others say Poe "escaped"). While he was out, Poe said, he lay down in the grass to clear his head, and when he returned, he was "much like his old self." He told Sartain that he had been wrong, that the whole thing was a scare created by his imagination. Soon after, he left, and Sartain never saw him again.

NORTHERN LIBERTIES

Although Sartain assumed that Poe had left the city, Poe had in fact made his way to George Lippard's printing offices. At this point, he was presumably in better health after harrowing

---

> "As it is myself who now tell you this tale—as you see that I did escape—and as you are already in possession of the mode in which this escape was effected, and must therefore anticipate all that I have to say—I will bring my story quickly to conclusion."
> "A Descent into the Maelstrom," *Graham's Magazine* (1841)

ordeals. There was a period of time, 10 days, Poe said, when he was delirious. He was imprisoned, he lost his satchel at the train station, he sought refuge with Sartain, and they went to the Water Works. It was not until July 12th that Poe surfaced at Lippard's. At this time, Lippard had his own newspaper, the *Quaker City*, a reform paper considered the first of its kind. Joseph Stevens and Company, located on lower Chestnut Street, published the paper. Some believe Poe

George Lippard
Library of Congress

sought out Lippard here, at the newspaper office, while others assume Poe went to Lippard's house, on North 6th Street in Northern Liberties.

At least one of Lippard's residences might still stand. Pictured here, on the far right, is the 6th Street home presumed to be his.

Poe's friendship with Lippard began while Poe lived in Philadelphia. When Poe worked at *Graham's Magazine*, Lippard worked at a daily newspaper called *Spirit of the Times*, which was located on 3rd Street between Market and Chestnut Streets just up the block from Poe's office.

Lippard was an incendiary social activist and best-selling author in his day. He is credited with forming the first labor union, the Brotherhood of the Union, which existed well into the 20th century. But before that, he published his breakthrough hit, *The Quaker City, Or, the Monks of Monk Hall: A Romance of Philadelphia Life, Mystery, and Crime*; his popularity soared with record-breaking sales. Just like

> "Well; you have heard, of course, the many stories current—the ⋯ⁿᵈ vague rumors afloat about money buried, somewhere he Atlantic coast, by Kidd and his associates. These ᴊmors must have had some foundation in fact."
> "The Gold-Bug," *Dollar Newspaper* (1843)

today, the more scandalous the better, and he stirred up plenty of controversy in his tale of urban immorality and greed based on current events. His story raised people's ire so much that on opening night of the play adaptation, the mayor urged Lippard to call off the production for fear of mob violence. Lippard relented.

An illustration from 1876, the centennial year of American independence. Its caption reads "The Tocsin of Liberty. Rung by the State House Bell, Independence Hall, Philadelphia, July 4, 1776."
Library of Congress

Philadelphia's claim to Edgar Allan Poe is not as well known as its claim as the "Birthplace of America," a nickname represented by the Liberty Bell. Legend has it that the icon of freedom and justice was rung for the reading of the Declaration of Independence. This tradition is thanks to Lippard, who wrote it in the 1840s.

Despite his colorful and significant contributions to Philadelphia and American history, he is often remembered only in Poe's shadow.

We learn of Poe's visit to Lippard from a letter Poe wrote on July 19th, from Richmond, Virginia.

> My Own Beloved Mother—
>
> You will see at once, by the handwriting of this letter, that I am better—much better in health and spirits. Oh, if you only knew how your dear letter comforted me! It acted like magic. Most of my suffering arose from that terrible idea which I could not get rid of—the idea that you were dead. For more than ten days I was totally deranged, although I was not drinking one drop; and during this interval I imagined the most horrible calamities....
>
> All was hallucination, arising from an attack which I had never before experienced—an attack of mania-a-potu. May Heaven grant that it prove a warning to me for the rest of my days. If so, I shall not regret even the horrible unspeakable torments I have endured.
>
> To L and to B— (and in some measure, also, to Mr. S) I am indebted for more than life. They remained with me (L and B—) all day on Friday last, comforted me and aided me in coming to my senses. L— saw —, who said everything kind of me, and sent me five dollars; and P sent another five. B— procured me a ticket as far as Baltimore, and the passage from there to Richmond was seven

dollars. I have not drank anything since Friday morning, and then only a little Port wine. If possible, dearest Mother, I will extricate myself from this difficulty for your dear, dear sake. So keep up heart.

All is not lost yet, and "the darkest hour is just before daylight." Keep up heart, my own beloved mother—all may yet go well. I will put forth all my energies. When I get my mind a little more composed, I will try to write something. ...

Poe wrote this letter six days after he left Philadelphia. Some of what he writes agrees with other accounts: his fear that Mrs. Clemm was dead, his 10-day period of derangement, and his sobriety.

The attribution of his insanity to sobriety is nevertheless curious. Without mentioning cholera, as he previously had, he states it was all a hallucination from an attack of *mania-a-potu*. The common definition of this type of mania is "a temporary, acute insanity, occurring in a drinker of neurotic temperament." A synonym for *mania-a-potu* is delirium tremens, which literally means shaking delirium, and occurs from alcohol withdrawal.

> When Poe lived in Philadelphia, 902 taverns existed in the city and county, just about one for every 100 people. At the same time, temperance and abstinence societies boasted memberships of 17,000.

"It was midnight; and you still sat by my side. All others had departed from the chamber of Death. They had deposited me in the coffin." "The Colloquy of Monos and Una,"
Graham's Magazine (1841)

Poe's use of initials in place of names is one example of the cryptic way Poe wrote. Some have theorized that Poe and other writers of the time wrote in code, decipherable only to the intended recipient, because of the competitiveness of the publishing industry; some have even said it was because they feared for their lives.

By cross-referencing Poe's letter with letters written by others, people have deduced that L was Lippard, S was Sartain, and B was Charles Chauncey Burr. The other men involved, whom we will hear about from Lippard, were Louis A. Godey, Samuel D. Patterson, and William F. Miskey.

Burr, the man who saw Poe to the train station, was a magazine editor who dabbled in mesmerism, or hypnotism, and phrenology, which was the study of the shape (not the size) of the skull. Phrenologists believed bumps or features on the skull indicated certain personality traits. The magazines Burr was involved with leaned more toward literature and politics. In fact, one of them, the *Old Guard*, was a pro-slavery publication that lamented the rise in numbers of abolitionists. T. D. English, Poe's foe from Philadelphia, replaced Burr as editor of the *Old Guard* in 1870. It is said that they agreed on everything except for

> Burr spoke out against Spiritualism, which was at the height of its popularity in the 1850s. He targeted the "rappings" of the famed Fox sisters as hoaxes. He and his brother demonstrated similar sounds by moving their toes in their shoes. Their endeavors were mockingly called "toe-ology."

> "Let me call myself, for the present, William Wilson. The fair page now lying before me need not be sullied with my real appellation."
> "William Wilson," *The Gift* (1839)

Griswold's slander of Poe.

In addition to helping Poe to the train that fateful day, Burr more than once came to Poe's post-mortem defense.

Likewise, Lippard's account, written years after Poe's death, gives us a heart wrenching and vivid picture of what happened when Poe came to him that mid-summer day in 1849:

> On a hot summer day, when the cholera was in the city, there came up four stairways, into a printing office, a slender man [Poe] poorly clad, and with but one shoe. There may have been genius written on his broad forehead, and the large love of a pure but neglected intellect in his clear eyes—but he was poorly clad, and with but one shoe to his feet. He came stealthily up stairs, as if conscious that the world had forsaken him, and that he was an intruder anywhere. He sat quietly down, near a table where a young man—an author [Lippard]—was writing. Then the poet—for the man shabbily clad was a poet—spoke to the author, and told him how he had no bread to eat—no place to sleep—not one friend in God's world. He besought the author not to forsake him.
>
> "You are my last hope. If you fail me, I can do nothing but die."
>
> You may be sure that the words which he spoke, and the voice in which he spoke them, went straight home to the author's heart. He had not seen the poet for some time. But he remembered how that poet had once a quiet

home, lightened by the smile of a wife—how he, the author, had often sat by him, and listened to him, as he poured out, free and unrestrained, the full thought of his heart. And the heart of the author sickened within him, to see a man like this, in want of bread—in want of a bed to sleep upon.

But the fun of the thing was, the author had just paid his last quarter's rent, and was without a penny in the world. He must therefore go forth, on that dreary summer's day, and endeavor to gain a few pence for the poet, from among the class who grew rich upon the labours of these beggarly devils—authors and poets.

"Tell them that I am sick. That I hav'nt a bed to sleep upon. That I only want enough to get me out of Philadelphia. Tell them plainly. For God's sake don't fail me. You're my last hope."

The author went out. Sick himself, and poor, he went from door to door, but everybody was out of town. It was a wretched day; cholera bulletins upon every newspaper door, and a hot sun pouring down over half deserted streets. The author was taken sick, and had but just strength enough to get to his own home.

Next morning, just after daybreak, he hurried down to the printing office, and found the poet there, sitting at the table in one corner, his head between his hands.

"I thought *you* had deserted me," he said, and tears came into his eyes. This was strange, for he was not the man for that kind of thing. Then he told him how he had waited there the day before—how he had paced those streets of Philadelphia, which, to the poor, are as full of hope as the hottest and dreariest piece of sand in Sahara—how the very heart was broke within him.

He also told how, before he came to see the author, the day previous, he had waited upon more than one person, whose eminence in literature was owing to his criticisms—and how these eminent persons had suffered him to wait in anterooms and offices, while their very lacqueys amused themselves by saying—"There's ———. He's drunk again."

"And now you're my last hope. Get me out of Philadelphia. For God's sake do it; I'm heart-sick for Virginia. I'm freer there, than in any other place. If I can only feel my boot upon Virginia sod, I'll be a new man."

The author heard words like these from the lips of the poet, and went out, and after some searching, found five men in Philadelphia, who agreed to give a small sum, in behalf of the poet. Three of these men were Magazine publishers. They acted like men. One was a clerk—he gave all he had—a dollar. Another was a man, who not only gave, but came to the printing office, and invited the poet to his home.

You should have seen the poet's face, when the author came back to the printing office, and told him of the success of his labours. There was a grasp of the hand—and a look of the face—which said much more than words. There was a tremor of the poet's lip, when the author told him of a certain publisher, who had refused to give one dollar.

"Not a dollar!" said the publisher, when he was asked. "Not a dollar."

The man who was with the author, (we need not tell his name), took the poet home, and the three spent the day together. That night those friends accompanied him to the cars, and saw him depart, after hearing his last words. They never saw him again.

But they never forgot, that saddest of all sights—a great man whose genius had enriched publishers, begging his bread in Philadelphia on a hot summer's day.

One day news came that the poet was dead. All at once the world found out his greatness. Literary hucksters who had lied about him—booksellers who had left him to starve—*gentlemen* of literature, who had seen him walk the hot streets of Philadelphia, without food or shelter—these all opened their floodgates of eulogy, and salvered with panegyric the man, whom living, they would have seen die in the next ditch without one effort to save him.

This is the joke of the thing.

One day the poet sits in a printing office—up four pair of stairs—one shoe to his feet—his only friend a miserable devil of an author, who is not only poor, but also an infidel—the next day the poet is dead, and from Maine to the Rio Grande the critics tune their pipes, and all the booksellers, the hucksters who *make* books for booksellers, the critics who live in perfumes, and write with gold ink on gold edged paper—all burst out into one long, loud ejaculation, "Great is the poet who is dead! Allah il allah! Allah bismallah!"

George Lippard, John Sartain, Charles Chauncey Burr and the others were the reason Poe made it safely to Richmond. Unfortunately, they were not present at the end of September.

"Diddling—or the abstract idea conveyed by the verb to diddle—is sufficiently well understood. Yet the fact, the deed, the thing diddling, is somewhat difficult to define. We may get, however, at a tolerably distinct conception of the matter in hand, by defining—not the thing, diddling, in itself—but man, as an animal that diddles." "Diddling Considered as One of the Exact Sciences," *Saturday Courier* as "Raising the Wind" (1843)

Angel of the Odd: Edgar Allan Poe's Last Days in Philadelphia

The tree-lined block between Poplar and Brown Streets on North 7th Street. Charles Chauncey Burr's home was located on "7th Street below Poplar," according to a Philadelphia directory, which was just one block west of Lippard's residence on North 6th Street. According to Lippard, he and Poe spent Poe's final day in Philadelphia at Burr's house.

"That the events of this narrative have hitherto lain *perdus;* that even the *fact* of the Rocky Mountains having been crossed by Mr. Rodman prior to the expedition of Lewis and Clarke, has never been made public, or at all alluded to in the works of any writer on American geography, (for it certainly never has been thus alluded to, as far as we can ascertain,) must be regarded as very remarkable—indeed, as exceedingly strange." "The Journal of Julius Rodman," *Burton's Gentleman's Magazine* (1840)

Chapter 4
The Angel of the Odd

From Philadelphia, Poe continued his lecture tour to Richmond and Norfolk, Virginia. By the end of August, a second wife finally seemed a reality with the most coincidental of possibilities: Sarah Elmira Royster, Poe's childhood sweetheart to whom he had already been engaged as a teenager. Sometime between his arrival in Richmond and the end of August, she accepted his proposal again. But there was a major caveat: she would have to sacrifice her late husband's estate.

In a letter written in late August, Poe tells Mrs. Clemm, who was still in Fordham, New York, of his intentions to return to Philadelphia to edit the poems of Mrs. Marguerite St. Leon Loud for a fee of $100. He also references his engagement to Elmira and ponders where they should live:

> ... The papers have done nothing but praise me before the lecture and since. ... I have been invited out a great deal—but could seldom go, on account of not having a dress coat. ... In a word, I have received nothing but kindness since I have been here, & could have been quite happy but for my dreadful anxiety about you. ... And now, my own precious

Mrs. Clemm, the very moment I get a definite answer about everything, I will write again & tell you what to do. Elmira talks about visiting Fordham—but I do not know whether that would do. I think, perhaps, it would be best for you to give up everything there & come on here in the Packet. Write immediately & give me your advice about it—for you know best. Could we be happier in Richmond or Lowell?—for I suppose we could never be happy at Fordham—and, Mrs. Clemm, I *must* be somewhere where I can see Annie. ... Mr. Loud, the husband of Mrs. St Leon Loud, the poetess of Philadelphia, called on me the other day and offered me $100 to edit his wife's poems. Of course, I accepted the offer. The whole labor will not occupy me 3 days. I am to have them ready by Christmas. ... I think, upon the whole, dear Mrs. Clemm, it will be better for you to say that I am ill, or something of that kind, and break up at Fordham, so that you may come on here. Let me know immediately what you think best. You know we could easily pay off what we owe at Fordham & the place is a beautiful one—but I want to live *near Annie*. ... Do not tell me anything about Annie—I cannot bear to hear it now—unless you can tell me that Mr. R. is dead—I have [got] the wedding ring.—and shall have no difficulty, I think, in getting a dress-coat.

"Be of heart, and fear nothing. Your allotted days of stupor have expired; and, to-morrow, I will myself induct you into the full joys and wonders of your novel existence." "The Conversation of Eiros and Charmion," *Burton's Gentleman's Magazine* (1839)

Angel of the Odd: Edgar Allan Poe's Last Days in Philadelphia

> In Poe's satire, "The Angel of the Odd: An Extravaganza," the angel of "odd accidents" and "improbable possibilities" visits a non-believer to convince him of the truth behind coincidences and strange occurrences.

It seems at this point, about two months after his strange experiences in Philadelphia, Poe was in a much better frame of mind. What with Elmira and good turnouts for his lectures, his only gripe seems to have been a need to live near Annie, Mrs. Richmond.

There were just two more (known) letters to Mrs. Clemm, the last one dated September 18th. In this one, he again informs her of his plans to stop in Philadelphia on business, stating, "On Tuesday I start for Phila to attend to Mrs. Loud's Poems—& possibly on Thursday I may start for N. York." He also confirms his feelings for Elmira, and hers for him: "Elmira has just got home from the country. I spent last evening with her. I think she loves me more devotedly than any one I ever knew & I cannot help loving her in return." At the close of the letter, he adds, "If possible I will get married before I start—but there is no telling."

If that were all, this letter would be unremarkable save for its optimism about the future. But this one also includes strange instructions for a return reply: "Write immediately in reply & direct to Phila. For fear I should not get the letter, sign no name & address it to E. S. T. Grey Esqre."

> "During the whole of a dull, dark, and soundless day in the autumn of the year, when the clouds hung oppressively low in the heavens, I had been passing alone, on horseback, through a singularly dreary tract of country..." "The Fall of the House of Usher," *Burton's Gentleman's Magazine* (1839)

Interestingly, if true, it was around this same time that Poe asked Griswold to be in charge of his literary estate should he die unexpectedly.

On September 27th, Poe left Richmond for New York via the Baltimore boat. He was planning to move Mrs. Clemm and their belongings to Richmond. It marked the end of the tour that began with his weird visit to Philadelphia.

According to Elmira Royster, Poe visited her the night before he left, complaining of being sick, but by the morning of the 27th, he appeared cheerful and healthy to his friends. Some chroniclers of Poe's last days believe he left some of his baggage behind in Richmond, either to make room in his trunk, or because he was in the beginning stages of a mental seizure. In either case, a trunk containing a lecture, papers to do business, books, and some manuscripts were located in Baltimore, either at the depot or at a hotel, after he died. According to some sources, Poe left with $1,500 cash in hand, either subscription money for his long-overdue magazine, or an advance for an article he was supposed to write.

No one knows for sure what happened between that point and when he was discovered in Baltimore on October 3rd. But some versions of the story take him to Philadelphia for a brief interlude before returning to Baltimore.

He reportedly arrived in Baltimore, from Richmond, on September 28th. From train records, scholars have calculated that he could have then arrived in Philadelphia either September 29th or 30th. Poe never made it to Mrs. Loud's to edit her poems, the reason for his stop-over here, as indicated by the preface in her book once it was published.

In fact, people have seen that non-event, as well as his aforementioned September 18th letter as evidence that he never made it past Baltimore. One Poe scholar dug through the records of the Philadelphia Public Ledger and found a listing dated October 3, 1849, for an unclaimed letter addressed to Grey, ESF. This find convinced him that Poe had not reached Philadelphia.

But James P. Moss, who lived on 4th Street between Chestnut and Walnut Streets, claimed to have brought a

4th Street between Chestnut and Walnut Streets is now the lawn next to and behind the Second Bank of the United States. In 1849, it was the location of James P. Moss's house.

"Out—out are the lights—out all! / And, over each dying form, / The curtain, a funeral pall, / Comes down with the rush of a storm, / And the seraphs, all haggard and wan, / Uprising, unveiling, affirm / That the play is the tragedy 'Man,' / Its hero the Conqueror Worm."
"The Conqueror Worm," *Graham's Magazine* (1843)

visibly unhealthy Poe back to his house on either September 29th or 30th.

Moss stated that Poe left them, still sick, the following morning. Moss believed that Poe accidently got on the wrong train, which took him back south to Baltimore, rather than north to New York. Others have speculated that Poe returned to Baltimore because of bad weather. Either way, a man discovered him outside a tavern in Baltimore on October 3rd. In just four days, Poe would be dead.

The Pennsylvania Railroad in the mid-19th century.
In attempting to retrace Poe's steps, scholars have pointed to at least three possibilities for Poe's departure from Philadelphia: the main train station at 11th and Market Streets, a sub-station at 6th and Chestnut Streets, or the ferry at Walnut Street. *Library of Congress*

"And the Raven, never flitting, still is sitting, *still* is sitting / On the pallid bust of Pallas just above my chamber door; / And his eyes have all the seeming of a demon's that is dreaming, / And the lamp-light o'er him streaming throws his shadow on the floor; / And my soul from out that shadow that lies floating on the floor / Shall be lifted—nevermore!" "The Raven," *American Review* (1845)

Angel of the Odd: Edgar Allan Poe's Last Days in Philadelphia

THE PREMATURE BURIAL

Poe was first buried in an unmarked grave in Westminster Church Cemetery in Baltimore just days after he died. Neilson Poe eventually ordered a tombstone, but it met an unforeseeable end when it was struck by a run-away train. In 1875, through fundraising and a donation by a Philadelphian, Poe's remains received a marker, but his birthday reads January 20th instead of January 19th. Mrs. Clemm's and Virginia's remains are buried with him.

When Joseph W. Walker discovered him (not in a gutter, as legend has it), Poe was wearing tattered, dirty, cheap and ill-fitting clothes, worn-out shoes, a straw hat, and he was barely lucid. He might have had with him an expensive cane, containing a sword. Walker sent for Dr. J. E. Snodgrass, who, along with Poe's uncle Henry Herring, brought him to Dr. John J. Moran at Washington College Hospital. There, Poe

> "In short, we are madly erring, through self-esteem, in believing man, in either his temporal or future destinies, to be of more moment in the universe than that vast 'clod of the valley' which he tills and contemns, and to which he denies a soul for no more profound reason than that he does not behold its operation."
> "The Island of the Fay," *Graham's Magazine* (1841)

went in and out of consciousness and never gained the wherewithal to tell Moran what had happened to him. He reportedly cried out the name "Reynolds," whose identity remains a mystery, and his last words were, perhaps, "Lord help my poor soul." Dr. Moran was the only witness to his death. Poe's cousin Neilson, the one whom Poe saved Virginia from so long ago, arranged Poe's burial for a day or two after he died, before Mrs. Clemm or Elmira were notified.

Poe's cause of death on record is congestion, or inflammation, of the brain. He was buried before an autopsy could be performed, and without those findings, people to this day remain unconvinced by the doctor's pronouncement.

During those mysterious two weeks in Philadelphia in early summer, Poe was in the grips of some kind of delirium. If his last visit in late September occurred, he was apparently unwell again. Based on these last two visits to Philadelphia, as well as other evidence, biographers have theorized that Poe suffered a chronic ailment, an illness left untreated.

A brain tumor theory surfaced quite recently when a writer revisited old documents from Poe's re-interment. Gravediggers reported they heard Poe's brain rattling around in his skull, and a sexton at the exhumation claimed that the brain was visible. Intrigued, the writer asked a coroner, who told him the claims were near impossible given that the brain is one of the first things to

> Different theories concerning Poe's death, in alphabetical order: brain disease, brain tumor, carbon monoxide poisoning, cooping, delirium tremens, diabetes, dipsomania, epilepsy, heart disease, heart failure, hypoglycemia, meningitis, murder, rabies, syphilis, and tuberculosis.

decompose. A likely explanation, according to the coroner, is that the noise they heard was a tumor that had calcified.

Still, if Poe's cause of death was a disease or ailment unknown and therefore untreated, would the doctor have written to Mrs. Clemm: "Presuming you are already aware of the malady of which Mr. Poe died..."?

One "malady" that followed Poe throughout his life was his relationship to alcohol. Coincidentally, the summer of 1849 saw Poe trying harder than ever to remain sober. He even went so far as to join the Sons of Temperance to show his dedication. In the letters Poe wrote during those two weeks in Philadelphia, he insisted that he did not drink one drop, excepting a glass of port wine, and he did say he suffered an attack of alcohol withdrawal.

> Along with John F. Kennedy, Marilyn Monroe, Amelia Earhart, and the Lindbergh kidnapping, Poe's death ranks as one of the greatest mysteries in popular American history.

There were reports, however, that when he arrived in Baltimore he drank with friends and then entered a state of delirium and madness. Similarly, Walker, the first on the scene, later stated that Poe was intoxicated when he found him. Nevertheless, Dr. Moran claimed Poe displayed no symptoms of alcohol consumption.

Some historians strongly believe it was murder—either premeditated or involuntary. In one favored scenario, Poe was caught in the middle of a political mess, as

---

"Between ingenuity and the analytic ability there exists a difference far greater, indeed, than that between the fancy and the imagination ... the ingenious are always fanciful, and the *truly imaginative* never otherwise than analytic."
"The Murders in the Rue Morgue," *Graham's Magazine* (1841)

Baltimore was notorious for political corruption. At the time, a type of voter fraud called cooping was very common. Political operatives would drug unwitting bystanders and force them to vote over and over again. Poe was found outside a polling place, on election day, in an area infamous for the practice.

> Researchers often wonder what Neilson Poe knew about his cousin's death after he reportedly insinuated to Griswold he had learned of new information. Unfortunately, he never disclosed what he had learned.

Interestingly, the train conductor reported seeing two men follow Poe once he got off the train at Baltimore. Were these two men set on drugging or perhaps mugging Poe? None of that $1,500—an enormous amount of money then—was ever found. Dr. Moran's initial opinion seems to follow this theory, as he claimed that Poe appeared to be beaten by thugs. Those who believe Poe carried the cane with the secret sword discount this situation, however, because they think Poe most likely would have used the weapon in self defense.

> Poe's romantic allure evidently reaches beyond the grave. On January 19, 1949, the night of Poe's birthday, someone anonymously left three roses and a bottle of cognac on Poe's headstone. The "Poe Toaster" was born. The tradition and the mystery continued until 2007, when Sam Porpora admitted it was a publicity stunt to raise money for the church. But the legend has taken on a life of its own, and people seem reluctant to believe Porpora.

Incidentally, it was during this same lecture circuit that Poe claimed to have been followed on the train from New York to Richmond. In Philadelphia, he stated the men were seeking revenge for a woman trouble. Had his troubles followed him? A witness in Baltimore claimed Poe was beaten up "by a ruffian," "at the instigation of a woman, who considered herself injured by him," a strange echo of his Philadelphia claims.

The ultimate cause of Poe's death will probably always remain a tantalizing—and maddening—mystery. Moreover, many skeletons came scurrying out of closets after he died, all adding even more layers to the story.

Rufus Griswold's resentment of Poe clearly ran very deep. In a bitter obituary signed "Ludwig" and published in the New York *Tribune* two days after Poe died, Griswold stated:

> Edgar Allan Poe is dead. He died in Baltimore the day before yesterday. This announcement will startle many, but few will be grieved by it. The poet was known, personally or by reputation, in all this country; he had readers in England, and in several of the states of continental Europe; but he had few or no friends; and the regrets for his death will be suggested principally by the consideration that in him literary art has lost one of its most brilliant but erratic stars.

Soon after, as Poe's literary executor, Griswold published the notorious biography of Poe in the preface of Poe's collected works. He even drew Mrs. Clemm into the scheme, offering her a certain number of copies of the anthology that she

---

"'You hard-hearted, dunder-headed, obstinate, rusty, crusty, musty, fusty old savage!' said I, in fancy, one afternoon, to my grand uncle Rumgudgeon—shaking my fist at him in imagination."
"Three Sundays in a Week," *Saturday Evening Post* as
"A Succession of Sundays" (1841)

could sell herself. She reportedly still had copies when she died, leading to speculation about the fairness of Griswold's deal.

When Griswold died in 1857, rumor has it that he had only three decorations in an otherwise barren room: portraits of himself, Poe, and Fanny Osgood.

As for Elizabeth Ellet, she perhaps could not let go of the past either. Right before Virginia, Poe's beloved wife, died, she blamed Ellet for driving her to her death by marring Poe's reputation. Strangely, Ellet was also blamed for "goading" Griswold to his death, which occurred seven years after Poe's.

Poe's allies banded together for their dead friend, determined to restore his reputation. George Rex Graham, Poe's former boss in Philadelphia, published his defense of Poe in *Graham's Magazine* in 1850, attacking Griswold's estimation of Poe's personality:

> I knew Mr. Poe well—far better than Mr. Griswold; and by the memory of old times, when he was an editor of "Graham," I pronounce this exceedingly ill-timed and unappreciative estimate of the character of our lost friend *unfair and untrue*. ... Among the true friends of Poe in this city—and he had some such here—there are those I am sure that *he* did not class among *villains*; nor do *they* feel easy when they see their old friend dressed out, in his grave in the habiliments of a scoundrel.

Other responses followed, either backing up Graham's view or perpetuating Griswold's version.

Charles Chauncey Burr published his opinion in his magazine, the *Nineteenth Century*, in 1852:

> I know that an attempt has been made by the enemies of Poe, to show that he was "without heart;" ...Poe was undoubtedly the greatest *artist* among modern authors; and it is his consummate skill as an artist, that has led to these mistakes about the properties of his own heart. That perfection of horror which abounds in his writings, has been unjustly attributed to some moral defect in the man. But I perceive not why the competent critic should fall into this error. Of all authors, ancient or modern, Poe has given us the least of himself in his works. *He wrote as an artist.*

Regarding the others with whom Poe spent his last months, either in person or in spirit, Sarah Helen Whitman was perhaps most successful in turning the tide of criticism. In 1860, she published *Edgar Poe and His Critics*, which was the first defense published in book form. Like the others, she defiantly directed her response to Griswold:

> It has been assumed by a recent English critic, that "Edgar Poe had no friends." As an index to a more equitable and intelligible theory of the idiosyncrasies of his life, and as an earnest protest against the spirit of Dr. Griswold's unjust memoir, these pages are submitted to his more candid readers and critics by ONE OF HIS FRIENDS.

Ironically, Poe's other fiancé, Sarah Elmira Royster, reportedly denied her engagement to him after he died. Instead, she claimed there was a "partial understanding" when he left her. Whatever understanding they had, to her, it meant she would never marry him "under any circumstances."

Nancy Richmond, perhaps in a symbolic gesture of alliance, reportedly changed her name to "Annie" following her husband's death.

George Lippard, Poe's friend from Philadelphia, published the following in the *Quaker City*, two weeks after Poe died, referencing Poe's visit to Philadelphia that summer and the years he lived here:

> Edgar Allan Poe died, in the city of Baltimore, on Sunday, nearly two weeks ago. He is dead and we are conscious that words are fruitless to express our feelings in relation to his death. Only a few weeks ago we took him by the hand in our office, and heard him express himself in these words—"I am sick—sick at heart. I have come to see you before I leave for Virginia. I am homesick for Virginia. I don't know why it is but when my foot is once in Virginia, I feel myself a new man. It is a pleasure to me to go into her woods—to lay myself upon her sod—even to breathe her air." These words, the manner in which they were spoken, made a deep impression. They were the words of a man of genius, hunted by the world, trampled upon by the men whom he had loaded with favors, and disappointed on every turn of life.

Poe spent a day with us. We talked of the time we had first met, in his quiet home on Seventh Street, Philadelphia, when it was made happy by the presence of his wife—a pure and beautiful woman. He talked also of his last book "Eureka," well termed a "Prose Poem," and spoke much of projects for the future.

When we parted from him on the cars, he held our hand for a long time, and seemed loath to leave us—there was in his voice, look and manner something of a presentiment that his strange and stormy life was near its close. His looks and his words were vividly impressed upon our memory, until we heard of his death and the news of that event brought every look and word home to us as keenly as though only a moment had passed since we parted from him.

We frankly confess that, on this occasion, we cannot imitate a number of editors who have taken upon themselves to speak of Poe, and his faults in a tone of condescending pity! That Poe had faults we do not deny. He was a harsh, a bitter and sometimes an unjust critic. But he was a man of genius—a man of high honor—a man of good heart. He was not an intemperate man. When he drank, the first drop maddened him; hence his occasional departures from the strict propriety. But he was not an habitual drinker.

As an author his name will live, while three-fourths of the bastard critics and mongrel authors of the present day go down to nothingness and night. And the men who now spit upon his grave, by way of retaliation for some injury which they imagined they have received from Poe living, would do well to remember, that it is only an idiot or a coward who strikes the cold forehead of a corpse.

If we will never know how Poe died, we can at least agree that his death was premature. One can only imagine what stories he might have concocted, what poems he might have written, what genre-creating and -bending he might have done had he lived past age 40.

A premature death is different than a premature burial, of course. The first implies youngness, something unfinished, or something lost. The latter, being buried alive, has somewhat different implications: horror and resignation, mistake and intention, life and death. Poe invoked both premature deaths and burials in his fiction and poetry, seriously and satirically.

We do not have to overlap what he wrote with who he was to recognize that although Poe is dead and buried, he is still alive.

Poe's literary legacy has weathered his strange afterlife, keeping him alive in classrooms, bookshelves, music, theater and film. New generations constantly breathe

"To be buried while alive, is, beyond question, the most terrific of these extremes which has ever fallen to the lot of mere mortality. That it has frequently, very frequently, so fallen, will scarcely be denied by those who think. The boundaries which divide Life from Death, are at best shadowy and vague. Who shall say where the one ends, and where the other begins!"
"The Premature Burial," *Dollar Newspaper* (1844)

life into his image and work, recasting the daguerreotype burned in our minds in new and exciting landscapes. For that, he is still alive.

Philadelphia played an irreplaceable role in Poe's life. Without Philadelphia, there would be no Poe as we know him. In a sense, his time here serves as a microcosm of his life. The six years he lived here, as well as the two weeks he returned, contain all the best and worst parts of him. This city saw it all.

Poe was buried alive. He is alive in his literary legacy. He is alive in popular culture. He is alive in Philadelphia.

Angel of the Odd: Edgar Allan Poe's Last Days in Philadelphia

A larger-than-life portrait of Poe watches over his home on North 7th Street in Philadelphia.

Angel of the Odd: Edgar Allan Poe's Last Days in Philadelphia

Acknowledgements

The Edgar Allan Poe National Historic Site, Philadelphia, PA
The Edgar Allan Poe Society of Baltimore, Baltimore, MD
The Free Library of Philadelphia, Philadelphia, PA
The Library Company, Philadelphia, PA
Tim Reeser
Eileen Reeser
Matt Ainslie

Bibliography

Bloomfield, Shelley Costa. *The Everything Guide to Edgar Allan Poe* Avon: Adams Media, 2007.

Buescher, John B. *The Other Side of Salvation*. Boston: Skinner House Books, 2004.

Burr, Charles Chauncey. "[I know that an attempt has been made]." *Nineteenth Century* February 1852.

Cirile, Cynthia. "The Mysteries of Edgar Allan Poe." 2007. 10th House Press. 27 Jan. 2009 <http://www.10thhousepress.com/index.html>.

Driver, Clive E. *Passing Through: Letters and Documents Written in Philadelphia*. Philadelphia: Rosenbach Museum & Library, 1982.

Eaves, T.C. Duncan. "Poe's Last Visit to Philadelphia." *American Literature* 26 (1954): 44-51.

Edgar Allan Poe Society of Baltimore. 11 Jan. 2009. Edgar Allan Poe Society of Baltimore. 27 Jan. 2009 <http://www.eapoe.org>.

Gibson, Jane Mork. "The Fairmount Water Works." *Bulletin*, Philadelphia Museum of Art Summer. 1998. *Philly H_2O*. 25 Mar. 2006. 31 Jan. 2009 <http://www.phillyh2o.org/backpages/PMA_TEXT.htm >

Graham, George Rex. "[My Dear Willis]." *Graham's Magazine* March 1850.

Hoffman, Daniel. *Poe Poe Poe Poe Poe Poe Poe*. New York: Doubleday, 1972.

Hubbel, Jay B. "Charles Chauncey Burr: Friend of Poe." *PMLA* 69 (1954): 833-840.

Hutchisson, James M. *Poe*. Jackson: UP of Mississippi, 2005.

Lippard, George. "[Edgar Allan Poe]." *Quaker City* [Philadelphia] 20 Oct. 1849.

Lippard, George. "Edgar A. Poe." *Weekly News* [Charleston] 3 Oct. 1853.

McMichael, Clayton, ed. *Philadelphia and Popular Philadelphians*. Philadelphia: The North American, 1891.

Neyfakh, Leon. "Poe's Mysterious Death: The Plot Thickens!" *New York Observer* 16 Oct. 2007. 27 Jan. 2009 <http://www.observer.com/2007/poe-s-mysterious-death-plot-thickens>.

Oberholtzer, Ellis Paxton. *The Literary History of Philadelphia*. Philadelphia: George W. Jacobs & Co., 1906.

Pearl, Matthew. "Mysterious for ever more." *Telegraph.co.uk* 23 May 2006. 27 Jan. 2009 <http://www.telegraph.co.uk/culture/books/3652541/Mysterious-for-evermore.html>.

Pettit, Edward. "We're Taking Poe Back!" *City Paper* [Philadelphia]. 2 Oct. 2007.

Quinn, Arthur Hobson. *Edgar Allan Poe: A Critical Biography*. Baltimore: Johns Hopkins UP, 1998.

Raymond Biswanger Slide Collection. 9 Jan. 2008. Rare Book & Manuscript Library Collections, U of Pennsylvania. 27 Jan. 2009 <http://www.library.upenn.edu/collections/rbm/photos/biswanger/poe-1849-philadelphia.html>.

Savoye, Jeffrey A. "Two Biographical Digressions: Poe's Wandering Trunk and Dr. Carter's Mysterious Sword Cane." *Edgar Allan Poe Review* 5 (2004): 15-42.

Silverman, Kenneth. *Edgar A. Poe: Mournful and Never-ending Remembrance*. New York: Harper Collins, 1992.

Weisberg, Barbara. *Talking to the Dead: Kate and Maggie Fox and the Rise of Spiritualism*. New York: HarperCollins, 2004.

Whitman, Sarah Helen and Oral Sumner Coad. *Edgar Poe and His Critics*. 1860. New Jersey: Rutgers College, 1949.

Woodberry, George Edward. *The Life of Edgar Allan Poe: Personal and Literary, with his chief correspondence with men of letters*. Vol. 2. Boston: Houghton Mifflin, 1909.